JEEPERS!

The Mystery of Simple Machines!

by Ailynn Collins

CAPSTONE PRESS
a capstone imprint

Published by Capstone Press, an imprint of Capstone
1710 Roe Crest Drive, North Mankato, Minnesota 56003
capstonepub.com

Library of Congress Cataloging-in-Publication Data is available on the
Library of Congress website.

ISBN: 9781669084587 (hardcover)
ISBN: 9781669084532 (paperback)
ISBN: 9781669084549 (ebook PDF)

Summary:
Join Scooby and the Mystery Inc. gang at a Renaissance Fair for an
adventure into the world of simple machines. Unmask the mystery behind
levers, wheels, pulleys, and more. Discover how these everyday machines
make life so much easier it's almost spooky!

Editorial Credits
Editor: Donald Lemke; Designer: Tracy Davies; Media Researcher: Svetlana
Zhurkin; Production Specialist: Whitney Schaefer

Image Credits
Alamy: imageBROKER GmbH & Co. KG, 5 (inset); Dreamstime: Bdingman,
29, Jay Dunbar, 28 (left), Kira Volkov, 5, Przemyslaw Klos, 4, Zhbampton,
17 (top); NASA: 25 (top); Shutterstock: AFM Visuals, 15, andrewtit,
6, antoniodiaz, 26 (middle), armi1961, 21 (biker), Artemiy_U, 25
(bottom), Artistdesign.13 (burst), 4 and throughout, berni0004, 16, 19,
BlueRingMedia, cover (pulley and cogwheel), 22, Boykov, 28 (right),
Cartooncux (beaker), cover and throughout, Crazy nook, 21 (dunes),
daseaford, 14, Designua (screw), cover, 24, Dina Milatina, 10, Frontpage, 13,
guillermo_celano, 23, HobbitArt (science icons), cover and throughout,
Honourr, 8, 9, LopezPastor, 20 (bottom), Lost_in_the_Midwest, 26 (top
left), Maria Martyshova (background), cover and throughout, Mintoboru
(gears), cover and throughout, Mirko Kuzmanovic, 11, 26 (inset), MK
photograp55, 20 (top), Net Vector, 30 (gears), Nigel Housden, 27, Noel V.
Baebler, 12, Oleksandr Panasovskyi, 18, Pedal to the Stock, 21 (middle),
Pixel-Shot, 24 (bottom right), Ronald Sumners, 17 (cheese), Sergey
Merkulov, 26 (bottom), Shchus, 24 (middle), sockagphoto, 24 (bottom left),
Steve Cymro, 7, trabantos, 20 (middle)

Printed and bound in the USA. PO 6121

Table of Contents

Mystery Machines

Scooby-Doo and Mystery Inc. have just solved a case at a Renaissance Fair! Like other fairgoers, the gang is dressed up as people from a time long ago. As they enjoy the fair, they walk past entertainers churning butter, lifting water from wells, and hauling wood.

Jeepers! That looks like hard work! I'm glad we have machines for those jobs nowadays.

Ruh-huh!

Guys, people long ago had machines too—*simple* machines!

A machine is any tool that helps make your work easier. (Just like the Mystery Machine helps the gang travel from case to case!) Machines lower the amount of force, or effort, needed to move an object.

Simple machines are, well, pretty simple. They usually don't have many moving parts. There are six types of simple machines: levers, ramps, wedges, wheels and axles, pulleys, and screws.

FACT

Work is the transfer of energy from one object to another. A machine is any tool that does work.

CHAPTER 1

Levers

OK, gang, let's start with levers! A wheelbarrow is an example of a lever. Have you ever used a wheelbarrow? If so, you know that this machine makes lifting heavy objects much easier.

Like, Scoobs, we need a wheelbarrow for all your Scooby Snacks!

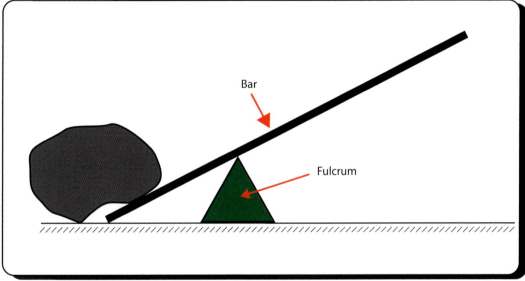

Bar

Fulcrum

A lever is simple, really. In fact, it's just two parts: the fulcrum and the bar. Think of the fulcrum as the anchor point, or pivot, which stays put no matter what. The bar is the part that moves when you push or pull on it. So, if you've ever used a stick to flip a big rock, you were using a lever.

FACT

To move or lift an object, force is applied to the wheelbarrow. Force is also called effort.

Like, hold the phone—there are three classes of levers! The type depends on where the fulcrum is located. In a first-class lever, the fulcrum is between the load and the effort applied. Chances are, you've used first-class levers and didn't even know it. . . . Scissors, seesaws, and pliers are all first-class levers.

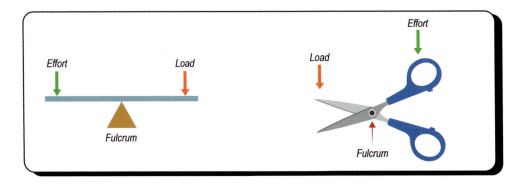

Remember that wheelbarrow? Well, it's an example of a second-class lever. With these types of levers, the load is between the fulcrum and the effort. Doors and nutcrackers are second-class levers too.

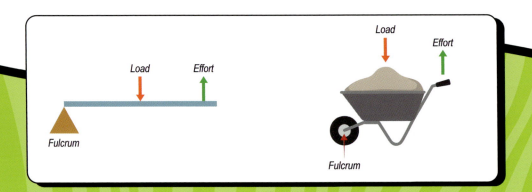

Finally, gang, we have third-class levers. With these levers, the effort, or force, is located between the fulcrum and the load. Shovels and barbecue tongs are great examples of third-class levers.

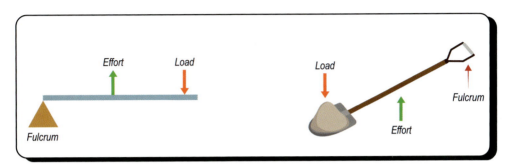

Effort   Load

Fulcrum

Load

Fulcrum

Effort

Like, did someone say "barbecue"?

FACT

Your arm is a third-class lever too! The fulcrum is your elbow, the load is the object you are lifting, and the effort comes from your bicep muscle.

All right, gang, let's get hands-on and build something fun: a catapult! This project will show you levers in action.

Building a Simple Catapult

THINGS YOU'LL NEED:

6 craft sticks
5 rubber bands
1 plastic spoon
1 Ping-Pong ball

BUILD YOUR CATAPULT:

1. Take three craft sticks and stack them on top of each other. Tightly wrap two of the rubber bands around each end of the stack.

2. Attach one craft stick to the bottom of the spoon with one rubber band close to the spoon's bowl.

3. Attach another craft stick to the spoon-and-stick stack with a rubber band in the middle of the spoon's handle.

4. Attach the last craft stick to the spoon-and-stick stack with the last rubber band at the end of the spoon's handle.

5. Slide the stack of three craft sticks between the bottom and middle craft sticks attached to the spoon.

6. Place the ping-pong ball on the spoon and press down. Release the spoon and watch the Ping-Pong ball fly!

This DIY catapult acts like a lever. When you push down and release, the spoon's movement transfers your effort, flinging the ping-pong ball across the room. *Ripee!*

What class of lever is this, do you think? Here's a hint. The fulcrum is located between the effort and the load. . . . You guessed it—a first-class lever!

CHAPTER 2

Ramps and Wedges

Gangway! Ramps and wedges are simple machines too. (FYI, they are also known as inclined planes.) They have angled surfaces, with one end higher than the other.

FACT

The tilted angle of an inclined plane is called the slope.

It's no mystery, guys. Ramps make walking uphill a lot less spooky!

Ramps make moving heavy objects from a lower level to a higher level much easier. Pushing something up a ramp takes less effort than lifting the object straight up.

A person who uses a wheelchair might use a ramp to enter a building. Furniture movers might use a ramp to haul heavy items into a truck.

Have you ever raced toy cars down a ramp? (If not, would you do it for a Scooby Snack?!) It's a great way to see inclined planes in action. The smoother the ramp, the faster your cars zip down.

But wait—! If you cover the ramp with sandpaper or cloth, the cars slow down. That's because of a force called **friction**.

Friction slows objects when they rub against each other. The more friction on the ramp, the slower the objects move.

Jinkies! Friction can be a real drag!

Like, stop slipping and sliding, Scoobs! We're about to be ghost toast!

Friction stops the movement of an object on the ground. **Gravity** pulls objects to the ground and adds to the **resistance**. Together, these forces can make work harder. *Ruh-roh!*

Without friction, people wouldn't be able to walk on the ground. Everyone would slide around as if walking on ice!

Hey, did you know that when you put two inclined planes together they make a sharp point? That's what we call a wedge! You've likely used one without even realizing it.

Wedges are great for splitting or separating stuff. Like, an axe is a wedge that chops wood. A knife is a wedge that slices food. And the teeth of your zipper? Yep, those are tiny wedges too!

Like, you nearly forgot about my favorite kind of wedge—a cheese wedge!

CHAPTER 3

Wheels and Axles

Next in line is the wheel and axle. This clever machine makes moving stuff a cinch! Picture a wheel with a rod right through its center (like a giant donut on a stick). When you give the wheel a whirl, the rod spins too!

Like, Scoob, you know why we love our van so much?

Ruh, why, Shaggy?

Because it's *wheely* easy to drive, even when we're chasing ghosts!

Since only the wheel touches the ground, it's the main fighter against friction. And because the wheel is lighter than what it's moving, pushing or pulling becomes a breeze.

Thanks to the wheel and axle, we can cruise in cars, pull heavy wagons, and glide on roller skates. And hey, your trusty bicycle? It's powered by this dynamic duo too!

FACT

Everything in the universe is matter. Matter takes up space and has weight. How much matter in an object is called its mass.

Look closely at a bicycle. Notice the chain and the gears between the pedals and the back wheel. Gears are wheels with tiny teeth around the edge. Bikes have gears. Clocks and windmills also have gears.

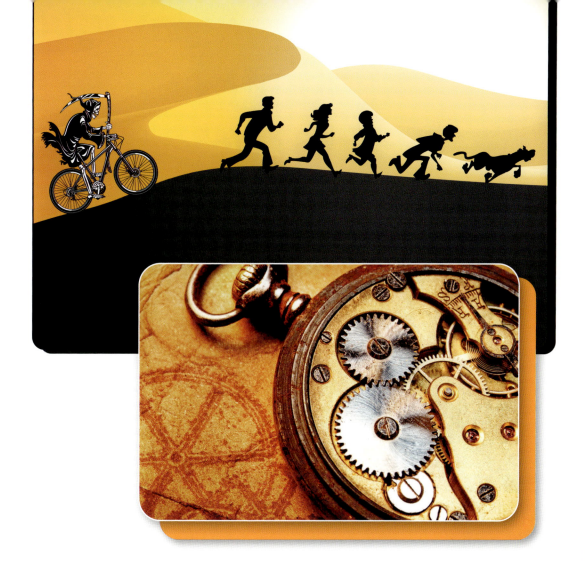

When gears are connected to each other, the movement of one gear moves another. When you turn a gear one way, it makes the next gear move in the opposite direction. When a large gear is turned slowly, it makes the smaller gear move quickly. This means that less effort is needed to do work.

Gears in a bicycle help the rider go uphill using less effort. Changing gears helps the rider to travel easily at different speeds and over different types of surfaces.

CHAPTER 4

Pulleys

A pulley is a simple machine that makes it easier to lift heavy objects off the ground. A pulley has a wheel with a groove along its edge. The wheel is attached to a fixed axle. A rope or cable is threaded along the groove.

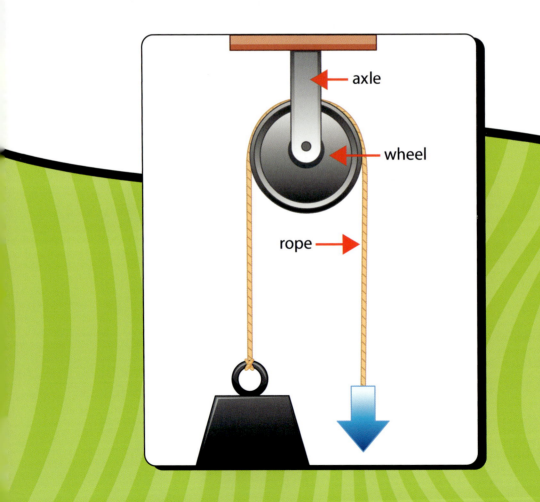

axle

wheel

rope

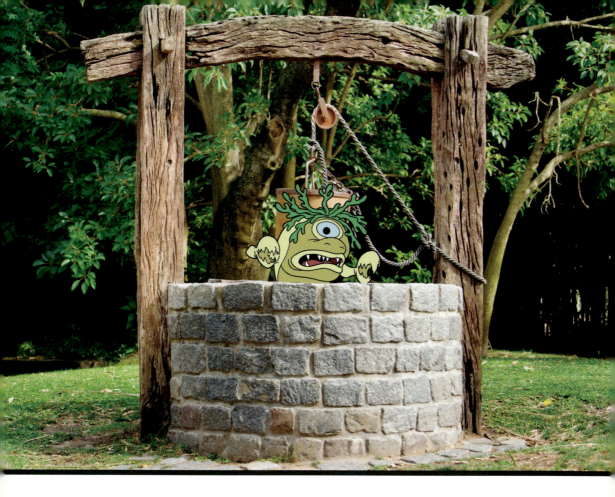

The object that is being lifted is called the load. When the rope is pulled, the load rises with less effort.

The more pulleys, the easier the work. The effort is shared by all the pulleys. It's easier to lift a heavy load with five pulleys than with just one.

FACT

A simple machine needs a force to do work. A door doesn't open until you push or pull it with force.

CHAPTER 5

Screws

A screw is a simple machine that holds things together. When you open a jar or change a light bulb, you are using a screw. The twisting force unscrews the lid off the jar.

Ridges
(narrow inclined plane wrapped around a cylinder)

Cylindrical shaft

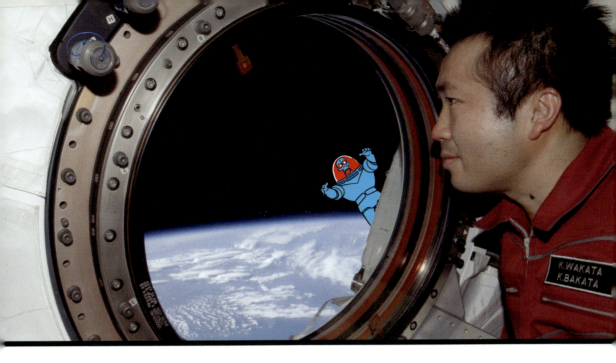

Screws are used to hold things together. Screws help when you are building furniture. They are even used up in space at the International Space Station. Screws can also be used to lift heavy loads as in a tire jack.

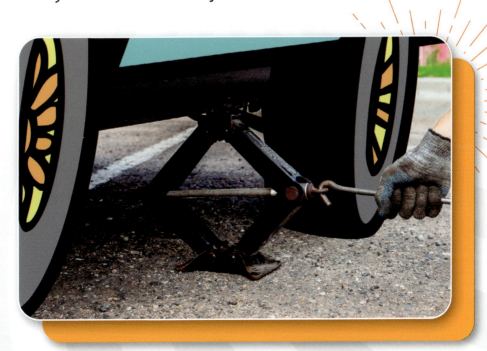

Drilling a hole into the wall to hang a picture is work using a screw. The circular motion of the screw is being converted into a straight line motion.

A screw's circluar motion can be used to transport water. Want to know how? Let's try an experiment . . .

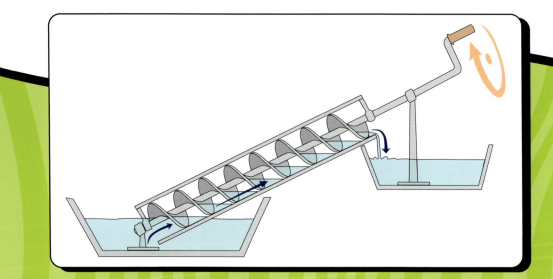

Build a Simple Screw Pump

THINGS YOU'LL NEED:

duct tape

clear tubing

small plastic pipe

scissors

food coloring (optional)

different sized containers

WHAT TO DO:

1. Using the duct tape, secure one end of the clear tube to the end of the pipe.

2. Wrap the tube around the pipe all the way along its length. Using the scissors, cut off the remaining tube and tape it to the end of the pipe. (You could also place tape in the middle to hold the tubing to the pipe.)

3. Fill a large, lower container with water. Add food coloring to make it easier to see the water's movement. Place a second, smaller container above the larger container. The second, higher, container should be empty.

4. Place one end of the pipe and tubing in the lower and larger container. Put the higher container at the other end of the pipe.

5. Twist the pipe and watch the water move upward into the empty container.

CHAPTER 6

Compound Machines

Not all machines are simple ones. When two or more simple machines work together to make work easier, they're called **compound** machines.

Many large machines are made of several simple machines. A bicycle is made of the wheel and axle in the pedals and wheels. The brakes are levers, and parts of the bike are held together by screws.

A wheelbarrow is made of an inclined plane, the wheel and axle, and a lever. Shoppers going up an escalator are using a compound machine. The moving staircase is made of pulleys and inclined planes. A car is a compound machine too.

Look around you. Can you find simple machines in the everyday things that we use? Who knows what mysteries and machines you'll uncover next!

Scooby-dooby-doo!

GLOSSARY

compound (KOM-pownd)—something formed by a union of elements or parts

friction (FRIK-shun)—a force that opposes the motion of objects when they rub against each other

gravity (GRA-vuh-tee)—the force that pulls objects toward each other

resistance (rih-ZIS-tuns)—the force that acts against the motion of an object

READ MORE

Edlund, Bambi. *Operation Cupcake: How Simple Machines Work.* Toronto: Kids Can Press, 2023.

Miller, Marie-Therese. *Simple Machines: A Sesame Street Science Book.* Minneapolis: Lerner Publications, 2023.

Schaefer, Lola M. *Lift, Mix, Fling! Machines Can Do Anything.* New York: HarperCollins, 2022.

INTERNET SITES

Ducksters: Physics for Kids: Simple Machines
ducksters.com/science/simple_machines.php

Generation Genius: Simple Machines
generationgenius.com/videolessons/simple-machines-video-for-kids

Science Buddies: Experiment with Simple Machines Science Projects
sciencebuddies.org/science-fair-projects/project-ideas/experiment
-with-simple-machines

INDEX

ABOUT THE AUTHOR

Ailynn Collins has written many books for children, from stories about aliens and monsters, to books about science, space, and the future. These are her favorite subjects. She lives outside Seattle with her family and 5 dogs. When she's not writing, she enjoys participating in dog shows and dog sports.